THE SPIRITUAL

TABLE OF CONTENT

1. Drake dream — page 2
2. Jay Z and Beyonce dream — page 2
3. Israel and Palestine dream — page 2
4. Cicely Tyson dream — page 4
5. Teachings – Knowledge — entire book
6. My Forbidden Lands — page 6
7. Scientists — page 8
8. Protesters – protest — page 10 – 15
9. Police Force Dream — page 14 – 15
10. Daughter, Poseidon/Hercules Dream — page 16 – 17
11. *Cost of 1 Sin for 7 Billion People* — *page 17*
12. Ancient Egypt Dream — page 18 – 20
13. My Frustration — page 21 – 25
14. The Annihilation of Earth — page 26 – 27
15. John Cena Dream — page 28, 46 – 47
16. *America, Barrack Obama Dream* — *page 28 – 40*
17. *Thoughts, Russia Dream, God Dream, WWE Dream +* — *page 41 – 61*
18. *Poetry* — *page 62 – 69*
19. Books by Michelle Jean — page 70

I so want to sleep right now. So cannot figure out my dreams. It's June 3, 2020, and on the second I dreamt this White Man under my bed. He seemed so alive with beautiful green eyes. I said something to him, but he said not a word to me. He just laid there as if he was dead. He had black hair, roundish face, and I would peg him to weigh about 180 – 200 pounds.

So yes, White Death is under my bed laying as if dead. Will not put anything toward this dream.

Now this morning I dreamt Drake the Canadian Rapper, me telling him about how nasty the bible is, especially when it came to the story of Adam and Eve but He Drake would not listen to me in the dream. He just walked away as if I was weird.

Drake dreams are usually death for me when he is with a male. Meaning, if I see Drake via my dream world with another male – Black Male high up, guaranteed a Canadian Male Rapper is going to die. But in this dream, Drake did not have a male with him, so I truly do not know. Will not analyze this dream. **_Yes, I was defending God, but this is me. Always defending God from the nastiness of man; men, and what they write about God._**

I also dreamt Jay-Z, and Beyonce. When I dreamt them, you saw the sky. **_The sky was White with a different hue._** I can't describe it. The dream reminded me of their net worth, **_and I said to myself in the dream; they are so poor spiritually._**

Yes, they are wealthy here on Earth but, in the Spiritual World; Realm they are truly poor. You will not comprehend Spiritually Poor, but I know the poverty associated with being Spiritually Poor.

I can't fully remember this dream, but I am not sure if the heavens; sky opened up and decimated Earth literally. I know destruction was there, but I cannot fully remember the dream.

As for Israel and Palestine, I dreamt about them, and I cannot fully tell you the dream. **_The dream had to do with conflict._** So, I am not sure if further conflict is going to brew in this region where an all-out war occur. So not going to worry about Israel and Palestine. **_The conflict there is truly not my concern, nor is it the concern of God._** Man; humans are evil; thieves, liars, warmongers, *and if a Nation of Vipers can lie on God, then they are truly not apart of the*

THE SPIRITUAL

<u>*Life and Kingdom of God literally. They are an enemy of the state; God literally.*</u>

Did I dream I was in the Realm of God?

Yes, but I cannot tell you the dream because I truly cannot remember it. All I know is, <u>*I was in God's Realm.*</u>

Spiritually speaking, I know the difference between the Physical and Spiritual. The physical is the physical, and the spiritual is the spiritual thus; **_THE COMPLEXITY OF LIFE._** Both realms are complex, and hard to navigate in so many ways. And yes, wrong wording on my part.

In a way, I know why when it comes to Earth, God is so weak. At times you do not get the true giving of God because, <u>*God is spiritual and not physical*</u> therefore, from a life perspective; Physical Life, and Spiritual Life is separated. And, I do not expect you to comprehend this even though we are physical, and spiritual beings. Therefore, **_Energy is complex._**

There is so much to know that it does take years for you to know. Therefore, <u>*time is not aligned physically, and spiritually.*</u> Spiritual Time is truly further in time.

The abundance of God's giving is truly not here on Earth but in the Spiritual Realm, and this is why many of us are dismayed; say God has and have failed us.

We cannot access the Spiritual Realm just like that and this is sad. Therefore, we cannot access our true getting. *The separation of male and female for those who are of a higher learning. Six-pointed Star*

In life, if you truly do not know, you will go around in circles, and you will get a headache. And yes, life is a bitch when you truly do not know. I am still finding this out the hard way because, **_there is so much lies you have to navigate through._** Not just lies in the Physical Realm but lies in the Spiritual Realm also. Thus, there is a lot that God truly cannot do. Cleanliness

Here in the Physical Realm truth is weak therefore, God is truly weak. There is an abundance of knowledge out there yet, the knowledge I seek I cannot receive.

The truth I need, I cannot receive. There is blockage on my part, and when you are blocked by Negative Energy and forces after a while, you want to give up and do give up. Therefore, life here on Earth is truly not for the good and true and or, those who are trying to live a good and true life. Life here on Earth is for the wicked and evil because true goodness; God is cut off from Earth. Meaning, Earth is governed – run by nasty people – the wicked and evil. So, because Earth is run by nasty and evil people – the wicked and evil; God cannot reside on Earth, or come into Earth.

Humans did make Earth the domain of Death – Physical Death.

So, the good we do here on Earth is truly not good but evil. No good can be good living in a world where it; the world we live in is dominated by evil. So no, God is truly not attainable here on Earth. When you are walking on the right path God truly do ignore your needs. *And yes, this is my negativity talking and or, speaking.* Yesterday was a day of hell for me where I did not care about life, or my life. But know. *For the good and true, God will always protect and guide you.* Despite the storms, God is with you, and in the storms with you. You just have to remember, after the storms come the calm. The Sun shines on you.

I did not care what happened to me because my life is one of loneliness at times, and the more death you see, **is the less confident you are.** Meaning, the more your world become insane to the point of depression for a day.

I do not know why you have to go through these phases in life where life matters not, and you want to tell God the F word again and again. The road to life is truly deadly because Death do not let you go. Nor does death let up on you. Death do all for you to break; cave in.

It's June 6, 2020 and for me June is a slow month – hell month because time is so slow that you have to wonder what is happening. It's like time is dragging its feet, and I do not expect you to comprehend this. Certain things you have to know feel, and if you do not know feel, and the way time feel, you will not understand, over stand, or comprehend what I am talking about. Yes, **you can feel time so, learn and know.**

Truly know how to feel. If you cannot feel, let God teach you how to feel.

So yes, I am in hell literally right now. Dreaming certain things that I cannot remember, and I truly do not care to remember. Dreamt Cicely Tyson and I were together walking. This Black Man; stout Black Man say around 250 pounds in a car; no, not car but jeep was sitting and watching her. Everywhere Cicely went he was there but neither Cicely nor I knew this. He also had a gun that he carried with him. Now his complexion is hard to describe. For me, I would call his complexion Muddy Black thus, his hue was different, **and hard for you to comprehend.** I can't remember what I did or said to Cicely, but he grabbed hold of her; Cicely and held a gun to her. I was trying to save her and so were other people but to no avail. Then all of a sudden, this Black Boy came which no one saw coming. He had a gun and he shot the Black Man that held Cicely hostage dead.

I am so not going to get into this dream because this is the second time I am dreaming about Cicely Tyson. So yes, **_death patiently awaits her literally._** Thus, I know her pain; hell literally because, I am seeing it.

Yes, there are different death's I know this but, **_I do not know why Death patiently waits for some in the living._** Yes, the life they live earlier on in their younger years for some, but it truly baffles me as to why Death wait on some so patiently.

So, no, you cannot speak of Life without speaking and or, talking about Death. Death is a true part of life here on Earth because none, not one of us can go back to God whole; as we are in flesh, and spirit.

So, as June is turning into a hell month for me, I just have to watch and see.

Been surfing the net; internet for cheap flights and vacation packages, and it's amazing how screwed up the internet is. **_If you as a human think your every move is not been recorded and watched, you had better think again._** Therefore, our world here on Earth is truly not private. **_Your basic rights and freedom is being infringed upon by those who own the internet._** Your government, and corporate giants – thieves – have to know your every move. **_We live in a world where you are being intruded upon to the point where I am so sick of man's so-called technology._**

There are times where I want; no, more than want, but truly need to create my own world where there's no people. No manmade crap or technology that infringe upon my right, and rights to life. Meaning, in my world, I truly would not care if humans kill themselves, act the fool, live out their evils, kill for death, do all the negatives – evils they can do to take self from life because, there are no humans just me.

Trust me, population growth would be limited. Meaning, in my world, **_outsiders would be more than banned from coming into my land._** Nope, don't want or need your diseases, tainted thoughts, tainted you, tainted anything. Therefore, many in Earth would be more than forever ever without end be truly locked out. **_And finding my domain and world would be more than impossible to find just like the Realm of God is impossible to find for billions._**

So yes, the knowledge of building to suit me eludes me.
The knowledge of curing my body with energy eludes me.
True happiness truly eludes me.

Outdated knowledge, thoughts; thinking, knowing on my part.

Listen, when you lack knowledge, your life is hell literally. It's like someone or something do not want or need you to find true knowledge; that limitless know where you are not dependent on the physical; physical knowledge. There is a beautiful world out there, and it's sad that I cannot truly explore it in the flesh; as I am. So yes, I am limited, and my limitations are shit because I cannot do what I truly need to do, and God is truly no help.

God do limit you here on Earth in my view thus, Earth is a containment unit; center; hub for Physical Death; the Death of Flesh. Yes, it sucks that our flesh have to wither and die, but then again, the sins of man – us as humans is truly not pretty but ugly. So, as June continue on its journey, I am truly not pressed for time, but I'm truly bored. June is too slow for me. I am so bored that I want to ride the train from one end of the city to the other to the way I am bored.

And no, the pandemic is shit but truly not getting to me. My boredom is different. I need to travel but being blocked from travelling. Cuba is the cheapest travel destination for me right now, but I truly do not want to do Cuba. Been there done that, and truly did not like my experience there; in Cuba.

Jamaica not approved of for me to go per God due to Jamaica being deemed unclean.

Namibia I cannot go, and this is my fault. So, God has banned me from going to Namibia. So yes, I am limited travel wise, and financially here on Earth. Trust me, if Jamaica was not banned for me to go to, I would be there right now soaking up the sun, and eating the mangoes; fruits of the land. So yes, my life is shit because I am being limited spiritually.

When God has forbidden you to go into certain lands, and you go into that land, you die spiritually. Thus, forfeiting life with God. Therefore, I tell you, *certain things we do is AUTOMATIC DEATH SPIRITUALLY once your spirit shed the flesh.* There is no saving grace for you because you went against a direct order from God.

When you go against God, your name is taken from of the Book of Life and put into the Book of Death. Absolutely no one can save you. Not even your precious Jesus if you believe in Jesus.

Not because God isn't here on Earth does not mean God cannot warn you another way. God is not physical, but it does not mean God cannot use energy; the energy of self; our self to communicate with us.

Dreams are one way Life; God, and Death communicate with you; us. Some people in the Black Community can see the dead face to face, and speak to the dead face to face. And, although our body shed the flesh, Death is spiritual also. *Meaning, our spiritual self have to; must answer for our crimes here on Earth.* So, the true death of humans is not here on Earth, but in the Spiritual Realm. Well on the Planet of Doom and Gloom as I call it.

And I am going to leave things here because; I am losing my train of thought. I am hungry; need my morning coffee, and I have to walk my dog though I don't want to.

Yes, my second child spoiled my morning. I so can't take the complaints about a dog anymore. Yes, I saw an apartment that is right; I can afford to live because the rent is really good. I truly do not mind relocating, and I am so going to relocate. I need it; need to relocate. I now have to find first and last month's rent.

Tired of grown ass kids complaining thus, I do not have true happiness in life.

Can't have true happiness in life. You have life the easy way yet, you complain about a stupid dog, what you do for me in this apartment, what you do for others, and more.

You complain about what you do in this house and I am truly tired of it. Tired of not being happy in life without the damn complaints. *I guess this is payback for me because, I complain to God so much.*

If things do not work out for me then that's okay. I just need to be away from it all.

Have to be away from my second's child company of friends that still feel the need to frequent my home during this pandemic. I know what this pandemic is, but give me and my house; apartment a break. But some Black People just feel the need to stress you out with their presence.

I truly do not like people coming to my apartment day in and day out. I truly love quiet. Hence, I need to create my own world; space where I truly do not see people every day. Truly an introvert, and truly anti-social.

So yes, the further I move from the T dot is the better it is for me. I will have true peace where I do not have to constantly see Black People; well my son's friends on a regular basis.

<u>At my age, I need my privacy, a quiet space; place, an environment where people don't constantly visit my home.</u> I need to live my way therefore, I am not that sociable when it comes to people, and the shit they do on a daily basis.

So yes, if I could have an island in the middle of nowhere where I do not have to see people regularly, listen to the complaints of people regularly, see the drunken state of some, a place where I can plant trees, fruit trees, food, have clean drinking water that is not dependent on the waterways of the rest of the world and more, I will be truly okay.

I have to have my own environment period.
I need a world of no cars, no confusion, no people; bothersome people.

A world of no church, no government, no corporations, no money – the different currencies of man, no technology; man-made technology, the different restaurants of men; humans, the different schools of lies and failure, and more.

On this day, God can be absent. Don't need God and the limitations of God. In my world God is truly not limited, God is limitless. So no, I truly do not need a God that is limited; weak.

Yes, no wonder I write because you can create a perfect world with words; your true and clean thoughts that are void of all evil.

Yes, it's a pity I cannot create a perfect world on Earth that is void of all sin and evil. A world void of the weakness and, the neglect of God literally.

A world where your problems – no, there are no problems because problems are non-existent in my world.

Death is totally shut out more than infinitely and indefinitely more than forever ever without end.

My garden is truly, and literally closed to all facet of death; evil. Nope, can't stand to see the ugliness of some who die therefore, no death is allowed in my world because, there is absolutely no evil; sin and evil in my perfect world. Just true clean living and creation, pure truth, honesty, true building, true harmony, ever growing cleanliness.

There are no diseases in my world either. <u>*Don't need any disease therefore, NO UGLY SCIENTISTS ALLOWED.*</u>

<u>*Scientists that create; design to kill are more than infinitely, and indefinitely more than forever ever without end banned. Scientists are DEATH'S PEOPLE so, Death can truly keep them literally without end.*</u>

<u>In my world, there is:</u>

No greed.

No fornication.

No illicit and explicit sex. Meaning, more than categorically no sexual misconduct; **_adultery._**

All must be satisfied sex wise, food wise, financially. Well there will be no greed of any sort in my world therefore, the use of money in my kingdom will be forbidden. Meaning, we have no need to buy and sell with others because we have all we need therefore, we are healthy, wealthy, wise, the true keepers of life, and more good and true things.

Yes, this is my perfect world, and I can write about it because this is what I do best; write despite the many mistakes in these books.

In my world there is no war, no crimes no form of evil, no breakdown of life, no illegal drugs, no depression, no mental instability of any kind, no mother and fatherless families, no stereotypes, no racism, no injustice, no evil whatsoever.

Parents will; have to take care of their children as well as, teach their children the truth of life. There will be no death therefore, we cannot and will never ever know death because there is absolutely no death in my kingdom; world.

Michelle

It's June 07, 2020 and I truly don't know where my head is at. Many protests going on with people taking the streets protesting Racism. I refuse to protest for anyone – especially those in the Black Communities Globally. We are too fool, fool in my view. Nor can you protest for justice in unjust lands.

I refuse to put my life on the line protesting for the unfair treatment of the other races towards Blacks anywhere.

I for one know that protesting is shit. Protesting do not work.

Those who protest are protesting for their unfair treatment to continue. Reverse psychology but people aren't seeing this.

Nothing will change in unjust societies yet, you have fools protesting they want change when change truly start with each individual.

How many have died protesting the ill treatment of Blacks Globally thus, I refuse to go on any Battlefield of Death; Evil to sway the treatment of Blacks.

Protesting is for the ignorant, and stupid; Fool, Fool in my book.

The only way to hit racist people is to stop supporting them economically in my view. Meaning, we as Blacks do not support racist businesses. Support our Black Businesses, and develop our own Black Communities financially like, *having Black Owned Banks, Schools, Hedge Funds, Insurance Companies, Grocery Stores, Hospitals, Televisions Stations, Radio Stations, and more that are truly independent, and not dependent on funding from White Society.*

In order for Black People to have justice, *we need to have our own good and true justice systems globally.*

We need to have our own Black; *GOOD BLACK OWNED NETWORKS GLOBALLY that are truly independent of White Owned Networks.*

In order for Blacks to have justice, *we need to be truly just to ourselves; each other. We can no longer cry wolf when it comes to injustice, and the unfair treatment of Blacks; us.*

We need to stop hanging on to the people, and systems that abuse us, and use us as guinea pigs.

It's time for us to stop protesting our own lies.

It's time we make a true change for us.

No stop.
No excuses.

PROTESTS ARE LIES.

PROTEST IS ANOTHER FORM OF REVERSE PSYCHOLOGY.

PROTESTS DO NOT CREATE CHANGE.

No, I said stop.

<u>Blacks need to stop fighting to be included in systems that were not designed for them.</u> You are Black. You are not White.

When the White Man and or, the White Race were designing their systems off the Backs of Blacks, you the Black Race was/were never included in their design – the White Race bigger picture.

You; Blacks were the Scapegoats, and still are the scapegoats – used and abused, the enslaved, and slaves.

We are the ones to make the White Race Globally <u>RICH OFF US.</u> See the designer cars, handbags, clothes, houses, gaming with gaming being sports, music, movies, entertainment, and more that we buy, get involved in, showcase, live in, and more. Also see, lands whites own in Black Lands, as well as see the downfall of the Black Race Globally.

How many of these stadiums; venues are Black Owned?
How many luxury hotels are Black Owned?
How many internet providers globally are Black owned?
How many Black Trillionaires, and True Billionaires are there?
Where is/are our Black – True Black Economy Globally?

Now going back to protesting for lies – to still keep you as Blacks tied to lies. What has changed given the protests and marches some of you as Blacks do? *See Martin Luther King Jr, Malcolm X, Marcus Mosiah Garvey, Nelson Mandela, and more.*

Stop forcing people to like you. It's my God given right not to like you so long as I am not hurting you, and inflicting harm on you.

It's time we as Blacks wake up and literally grow up.

How the hell are you going to protest for change when we literally have nothing for our self to call our own? <u>*NOT EVEN GOD WE HAVE PERIOD.*</u>

Don't even go there because, billions in the Black Community Globally praise and worship including, bow down to a White God.

<u>*IN ORDER FOR US TO HAVE CHANGE THAT IS FAIR AND JUST, WE NEED TO CHANGE CORPORATE, AND GOVERNMENT LAWS.*</u>

<u>*Without Corporate laws changing.*</u>

<u>*Without the laws of the government changing on/in all levels of government to include, and be fair to Blacks, protests will never work because; the key factors – elements that design, and promote – implement Racism, and Systemic Racism is still there; have not changed. Therefore, we as Blacks cannot, and will never have change in societies that are not designed for us.*</u>

Therefore, we protest; are protesting a losing battle. <u>*YOU CANNOT FIGHT THE DEVIL WITH THE DEVIL'S OWN AGENDA.*</u> You are stupid when you do so. The blind leading the blind without a guide dog, or a guide stick.

Listen people, it's not every Black Person that want to see their own Blacks succeed. You do have Blacks that profit; benefit off/from the demise of their own Black People. They play the game – Black Game because we allow them to. Therefore, many do not elect <u>*GOOD BLACKS TO OVERSEE THEM;*</u> implement laws that not only benefit Blacks, but all in their community fairly; just.

<u>*Onwards I go.*</u>

Look at how we make other nations rich off us.

Rock your natural Black Hair.
Rock Black Designer Clothing.
Rock our own Black Skin.
Support Black Books.
Support Black Theatre.

Support Black Films that are Black Written, with Black Casts.
Support Black Made – owned make-up companies.

Go to all Black Schools that do not fall under White jurisdiction – the White School System - curriculum.

Support Black Radio.
Donate to Black Radio.
Travel – vacation in Black Lands.

When you travel to a Black Land, bring a backpack, a pencil, eraser and give it to a Black Child. See where I am going with this? Let your true blessing flow on you come on now. We can build us. It is us that truly do not want to build us positively.

Black society is good. It is us as Blacks that refuse to build up Good Black Societies that are not based on White Lies – White Society.

We as Blacks need to truly diversify our Black Portfolio to include Africa and the Caribbean. Therefore, Black Countries need to make it affordable, and less restrictive for us as Blacks to visit, travel to Black Lands but then, the hotels are White Owned go figure.

I've told you in other books. <u>THE WHITE MAN'S GOD IS TRULY NOT THE BLACK MAN'S GOD.</u> Therefore, as Blacks, we should not bow down to death, and the lies they tell us come on now.

Anyway, I am so not going to get into all of this because I am repeating myself from other books. *HOW THE WHITE RACE KILL BLACKS IS TRULY UP TO THE WHITE RACE. WE AS BLACKS REFUSE TO BREAK AWAY FROM THEIR LIES; WHITE LIES, AND UNCLEAN LIFE AND LIVING; WHITE SOCIETIES GLOBALLY.*

As Blacks we fail to realize that when we give up life; death is all you have, and many Blacks have and has chosen Death as their god. So, however we are used, abused, killed, we as Black should not complain because many in the Black Communities Globally did chose Death for self.

Listen, once the protest is over, Blacks will go back to their ignorant and non-caring ways therefore, going right back into the shit they claim is affecting them.

I refuse to be like everyone. **HUMANS ARE RACIST PERIOD.**

IT IS MY RIGHT TO BE RACIST. IF I DON'T LIKE YOU, I TRULY DON'T LIKE YOU. <u>IT'S US AS BLACKS THAT REFUSE TO LEAVE OUT OF RACIST LANDS.</u>

Sum a wi kill wi self to go live in racist lands. Therefore, Black Lands are truly not Black Owned. *Our corrupt and crooked politicians made it so; sell land, and people out.*

Our Future Generations need a future yet, *the same crap of shit that truly do not like us, have huge investments in Black lands therefore, raping our future Black Kings and Queens of their legal rights future wise.* You don't like Blacks, don't sell to Blacks. Say these products are not for Black People. *FOR WHITE PEOPLE ONLY.* It is your right, and I cannot hate you for this. It's not racist, my product is not for you period.

If you don't like me, don't buy my books and or, these books period. It's nothing against you, these books are truly not for you. *So White People, when Blacks say, no Whites, or other Nations allowed, don't be upset.* *We have a right not to want you in our world; Global, and Godly environment period.*

So yes, I will forever petition God against the Sell Out Blacks of the Globe. Mek dem nyam shit for all I care. Wi too frigging stupid. Thus, Blacks are the puppets, scapegoats, and guinea pigs for other races.

Wi ha di bess hair any race can have, and many truly do not like their kinky hair. They would rather rock haase batty, and go bald before they appreciate their true crown of life that God has, and have given us; them.

Many are so tattooed that they don't know they've sold their soul to the Death literally. *The Mark of the Beast.*

Some bleach their skin like dyam fools thus, White Psychology has and have brainwashed many in the Black Community. An wen yu talk, many Blacks hate you because they truly do not know what it's like to be Black; have true ancestral roots.

Blacks were never like this hence, OUR TRUE ROOTS WITH GOD THAT WE HAVE AND HAS FORGOTTEN. And yes, some has literally forfeited.

So yes, we as Blacks live in lies.
Die in lies hence, *Death love us so.*
Protest to stay in lies.

We do all for Death instead of doing all for self – our life.

As I said, it's June 7, 2020, and my dream world, I truly do not know what to make of it. I am seeing Bloodshed in the Police Force. In the dream, ***the agenda is and or, the command that was sent down from the head of the Police Force is to eliminate Good Police Officers.*** So, whatever is happening in the United States with their Police Force is nothing new for me, and to me. It's not the first time I am dreaming about Good Cops being eliminated so that the force; Police Force is overrun by corrupt cops' period. And none of you better come to me and say, you are racist. It is my God given right to be racist. I don't have to like you, and you do not have to like me.

AS LONG AS I DO NOT INFLICT HARM ON YOU, SPREAD HATE, TELL OTHERS TO HARM, AND HATE YOU, I AM GOOD TO GO.

I refuse to stand up and fight you. *I HAVE MY TRUE DEFENCE IN GOD THEREFORE, GOD IS WHOM I TURN TO FOR SOLICE, AND NOT DEATH.*

GOD IS MY WEAPON AGAINST YOU PERIOD.

Michelle

This one particular dream is long, and I will not get into the dream in full length. The dream had to do with my daughter, where my father lived, and them building new condominiums in his area, and on the same building he lives in. Beautiful condominiums. White builders, and building faulty. One builder that was working on the building pointing out the faults of the building, and saying, the person that did this will be sued, this Black Man with faulty shoes on that was going in the same direction of where I lived but, hesitant to give us; me and my daughter a ride home.

He was mean people.

This is where the dream took a turn for me. I saw this young White Guy say in his early to late twenties jumping into the water, and another guy jumping in the water to save him – the one that initially jumped into the water, and the hand of death reaching out to take his life – the one that jumped into the water initially, and me telling death to stop. Do not take the young man's life. **_In the dream, I had the power to stop Death._** And in the dream Death was Poseidon with the colour of Blue. On his finger he had a ring, and a black strap on his hand.

Poseidon did not like me stopping him. Anyway, his hand was thrown away. But Poseidon had a child. Little girl child made of silver; all silver, and she had a bald silver head. She was given the hand of Poseidon. And I thought she might turn because Poseidon was her father. After that Poseidon's daughter around age 6-8 no older was walking with Poseidon's hand. Then, I was with a very young Hercules. When I mean young, I mean young, and promiscuous. He was not allowed to have sex at a young age, but he was having sex in baskets with the older girls; white girls. This one Black Lady that was not attractive, he did the nasty with; had sex with her. When she realized he/Hercules came on her vagina area, she made sure his white ejaculative fluid got into her vagina. So, she became pregnant for Hercules, and men with spears sought to kill the child; bi-racial child of Hercules. Trust me, Hercules wasn't having it; someone trying to kill his child.

So, I truly do not know who is building faulty in Canada, Jamaica, the Globe. Nor, do I know if the waters of life is going to turn against man. Meaning, I do not know which land is going to get flooded with water. With me stopping Poseidon; Death, death is angry. So, which land Death is going to ravage I truly do not know. And with Poseidon's daughter walking with her father's hand in her hand, I truly do not know which land she is going to destroy. **_So yes, death is in the water, and death is on land._** Plus, I truly do not know what Greek Mythology represent in my dream world. This is the first time I am seeing Poseidon, nor do I know why Death would represent himself as Poseidon apart from, the power and strength of Death. I know Spiritual Death and or, Final Death is White, but the use of Greek Mythology is beyond me. And Hercules having a bi-racial child is weird. The bi-racial child can only be The Christ – Jesus that so many globally worship and praise plus, say is God.

I had other dreams as well. Some I cannot remember, and some I can.

Need to get me some ginger and turmeric tea as well as, Ganja tea. Organic tea. Do not need the chemical shit that we are given globally.

There is this force out there that I am connecting with, and for me to be able to stop Death again is telling me something. You will not comprehend this, but I know.

So yes, the Spiritual Realm can be weird; different. But I am not going to worry about the Spiritual Realm, nor am I going to worry about the happenings in Greece. Those that have eyes can truly see; know what is to come shortly.

I am in the Realm of Death; Physical Death. Death here on Earth is nothing like Spiritual Death. Spiritual Death is where you are consumed by fire – the fire you created for self with your sins. Therefore, many truly do not think of the next phase in life once your spirit shed the flesh.

Listen, I cannot worry about the sins of man. If you do not worry about you, why should I worry about you. I don't even know you.

It's the same with God. Why should God worry about your sins when God truly do not know you? Yes, Death know you because all you do here on Earth is of Death. You do for Death so yes, Death have to love you. You prolong the life of Death in the Physical, and Spiritual Realm.

See the sins of each individual here on Earth, and the cost associated to/with 1 sin. For example, in simple terms, the cost of 1 sin is:

$48000 \times 24000 = 1\,152\,000\,000$ years in your hell.

Now there is over 7 billion people here on Earth not including those who have died already. Now multiply 7 billion sins by $1\,152\,000\,000 = 8.064e+18$.

Which is $8\,064\,000\,000\,000\,000\,000$. This is the number of years death stays alive in the Domain of Death for just 1 sin for 7 billion people. Now compute the rest of the sins, humans do including, compute the sins of those who have died. Therefore, Death has numberless years to live in the Realm of Death due to humans literally.

<u>So, if you are not of Life, God cannot save you. Will never ever save you.</u>

Michelle

I don't know what the Spiritual Realm need me to know when it comes to the past civilization of Black People.

Dreamt I was in the past. I was in Ancient Egypt, and I was eating grapes, sweet grapes that was delicious. Tasty and juicy.

Apparently, there was this Black Man that was deemed dangerous. I do not know if it was because of his knowledge he was deemed dangerous but, deemed dangerous anyway. I was telling the people; those that were around me – all Black People about how you have Babylonian Indians saying there were no Black People in Egypt.

I will not put any emphasis on this dream, **and as to why I was telling Black People in the past what was happening in our day and time.**

See in Egypt there were only Black People. There were no Whites, Chinese, or Indians. Thus, Blacks have and has lost their way, culture, identity, life, land, educational systems, and values. Therefore, you have grave robbers raping the dead in Egypt of their life – resting place, and thieves that do not belong in Egypt living there, and claiming our identity, true life of the past as theirs.

So yes, Blacks throughout history – our life story, past has and have lost it all; our identity to identity thieves. Blacks of the past and today are losing it all. **Not even our past accomplishments are safe because thieves literally rob us of everything.**

Yes, we are at fault because as Blacks we do not teach the truth to our children. Nor do we protect what truly belong to us.

Instead, we rely on the educational systems of liars – our colonial slave masters to educate us.
Therefore, we have no true life lessons to bring forward; teach our future generations. We keep adopting the lies of other nations while they reap the reward of our greatness, and our great accomplishments.

Where are our own museums that house our ancestors of the past?

Museums that showcase Black Accomplishments.

Black Design
Black Inventions
Black Travel
Black Clothing
True Black Life

THE SPIRITUAL

Nope, we are to let the dead rest and not bother them. *Our dead can reach us and teach us; educate us on certain things.* But, when you have thieves disrespecting our ancestors

Burial Rights; our dead cannot teach us anything nor, educate us, warn us, or protect us. Therefore, we truly do not need to interfere with the dead. We can connect to those that have lived thousands of years before us, as well as those in the beginning. It is us as Blacks that has and have forgotten what we can and cannot do spiritually.

So, Egypt I will leave alone because no matter how thieves steal our culture, and truth of our civilization of the past, our ancestors do, and will find a way to remind us as Blacks of our true life of the past.

So, no, as true Blacks we cannot forget our ancestors of the past. The smarts of them has and have kept us going no matter the lies we are given. Somehow the truth will keep on resurfacing of what life was in the past when it comes to us as *TRUE BLACK PEOPLE.* Yes, it is sad that there isn't a true Black Curriculum that is in the different schools globally that teach us/Blacks about our greatness so that young, and old can stand proud of the things we did from then until now.

We no longer have great leaders that we can look forward to because everything for Blacks is tainted by the different races.

Blacks have adopted the lies of other civilizations that have absolutely nothing to do with Black People.

We refuse the truth therefore, many Blacks Globally are living in lies – the dysfunction of others including family dysfunction.

Other races dumb us down, thus we've become ignorant of, and to our past accomplishments.

Every civilization has and have benefitted off Black Culture, Black History, Black Thought, Black Civilization, Black Life, Black Everything. And when you talk, speak the truth in today's society you are deemed as racist. *NO ONE CAN BE RACIST FOR THE TRUTH.*

The society we live in, you cannot think this way, or that way. They; them that govern must do the thinking for you.

As Blacks we need to see our accomplishments, and set good values for self, and our community including children; family. When we start truly loving our self, truly accepting the fact that we have no limits as long as you know how, then maybe we can see ourselves in life. *Not the life they tell us, but the life we will come to know.*

Like I've said in other books, *we can write our own life story with God,* it is us as Blacks that refuse to do this. We've become so complacent in the lies we've accepted that we've forgotten that God has always been there for us.

God has been trying to educate us on life, it is us that refuse to listen. We want things our way all the time. I do at times. Despite what I write, cuss out people, *VALUE YOURSELF; YOUR LIFE BECAUSE YOUR LIFE IS WORTH IT.*

It is those people who have no worth in life that do all to keep you from succeeding.

For those who control this Earth; *THE TRUTH MUST NEVER BE KNOWN. If you know not the truth you cannot live, nor can you achieve God.*

Those who cover up the truth are Death's People literally. They have no worth, or self-worth in life. Thus, they have no life with God. All they do is please death thinking Death is going to secure their life when, Death cannot secure the life of anyone. *Death can only kill you.*

The sole purpose of Death is death and nothing else.

TOMORROW by Pieter T featuring Tyna

For many they think they do not have a tomorrow, but there is a tomorrow. Absolutely nothing can end tomorrow. Everything have to; must end today therefore, absolutely no one can die tomorrow. They can only die today. Tomorrow turn into today people.

So, make your life have worth today. Tomorrow is guaranteed it is us as humans that take our tomorrow from us. So no, *no one can live tomorrow, they can only live today.*

I am so not going to get far into this book. Things are day by day for me. Going to add some poetry in this book. I need to branch out just a bit.

Truly hope you will like my poetry.

Listen, darkness do(es) not have to be. So, truly know you.

GOD IS GUARANTEED FOR MANY, BUT FOR BILLIONS GOD IS TRULY NOT GUARANTEED LITERALLY.

Michelle

God how I loathe Microsoft and their bullshit.

Man's technology is pure stress and heartache.

Microsoft stinking, jacked up, corrupt, intrusive, invasive spy crap of technology has and have locked me out of my laptop due to their lousy, stinking shit hole of an update that has and have changed my login password.

Lovey, do we truly need crap of technology – man's technology that spy on you, and rob you of your happiness literally.

God, you don't know how I truly loathe Microsoft and their bullshit.

Is there not a better way in life?

Yes, I truly loathe man's so-called tech – no, deathnology/deathtology that contribute to your pain and suffering here on Earth.

Michelle Jean
June 12, 2020

No Lovey, I am so frustrated and sick of the White Race of idiots that frustrate my life, and the life of others.

June so far has been my Month of Hell.
Frustration
Loathing
Crap

I began to write poetry and have to stray from it because some asshole in the universe has and have turned up the forcefield of negative energy around me here on Earth.

What the hell is wrong with these shegging negative forces?

Leave me he bleep alone.

Now the Moon is running from me.

No Lovey, I truly have an issue with people especially those evil ones that benefit; profit off cheating, and deceiving people.

Why the hell can't their hell; these damned crooks – corporate liars, evils and sins not turn back on them here on Earth?

Why cause me pain Lovey?

Michelle Jean
June 12, 2020

No Lovey, it's not all White People that are hogs of the worst kind here on Earth. But I am truly, and literally tired of them; the White Race; White People in hue; whether the hue is Black, Brown, Pale, White whatever.

You know what Lovey, I truly hate; no, loathe technology; deathtology/deathnology.

Yes Lovey, man's so-called technology is death.

I truly don't need or want it because technology; the deathtology/deathnology of Man is truly unclean.

The White Man's technology spy on people. **<u>Break our fundamental human rights.</u>**

It saddens me that we as Black People cannot have our own good and true technology that do not spy on people. But then again; knowing how naïve we as Blacks are, we would teach White People our technology and they; Whites would take credit for our achievements. Just as how we teach them to dance; have Black Rhythm. <u>Afro Beats</u>

Michelle Jean
June 12, 2020

Lovey, it's June 12, 2020.

Let me ask you something.

With this Pandemic, *how many medium size businesses have closed permanently?*

Yet, the major corporations of the globe, and banks have gained; recorded profits.

How many lives have been shattered yet, the rich and super rich are still gaining?

This Pandemic was created to bankrupt medium and small business even governments yet, the superrich, and rich is still gaining.

Why Lovey?

Why are so many corrupt here on Earth? **White Collar Criminals**

Why do the evil ones gain yet, the simple man; person that is trying is dumped upon?

When will the greedy few crumble, and lose it all Lovey?

When will the greed of the corrupt come to an halt; true end Lovey?

Yes, I know not all is over, but why is the 1% of the globe so corrupt; evil Lovey?

Do they not think of hell; their hell?

No, soulless people cannot see hell, nor do they know their own hell.

Michelle

Aye Lovey, the Moon is gone.
The Moon is gone
Gone from me

Running
Running
Running

The Moon is gone Lovey.
What can I do to bring the Moon back?

What can I do to make the Moon stay?

Continually shine its light on me.

The Moon is gone Lovey.
The Moon is gone from me.

How do I get it back?

Why does the Moon run from me?

At times hide from me for the longest while.

Aye Lovey

The Moon
The Moon
The Moon

Do take care but, bring back my baby truly close to me.

Michelle
June 2020

It's June 13, 2020, and I truly don't know what is going on with me.

My nights are truly painful.

Pain has escalated to the point where I cannot bare it. Had to take 2 Acetaminophen 500mg to try to alleviate some of the pain I am feeling. Hate taking pain killers, but you know I could not bare the pain for me to take them.

Pain wise my life is truly not pretty.

Body lock up sometimes.

Can't even sneeze without my body locking up and causing me pain. Even my bones feel painful. Truly do not wish my sufferings on anyone.

Shoulder pain is a bitch because I can feel a lump in it.

Pain is hell therefore, I am suffering in the system I am in. Too much pain that I have to go through.

But through it all, I have to have hope. Do what I can to prolong my life here on Earth until I can be in the environment I need to be in where I do not have worry about pain and suffering – the total decay of my physical, and spiritual life.

I need an environment that is warm where I can walk, absorb the natural sun, plant truly organic food, drink fresh and clean water, and more.

Okay enough about me.

I truly do not know why I am seeing the total decimation of Earth. Just now, well not too long ago, I saw the annihilation of Earth. **_It's as if I keep dreaming about the annihilation of Earth but, there is no dream for me to remember._** It's as if I am seeing this annihilation before me without knowing about it if that makes any sense.

It makes sense to me, but I don't think it makes sense to you.

With what's happening globally with this Pandemic, the Annihilation of Earth truly do not surprise me. I welcome the Death of Earth. Humans are truly too wicked when it comes to each other.

As for my pain, I do not know if it's the Pain of Earth I am feeling. If it is, Lord help me because her pain is truly painful. But, I know I am not feeling the pain of Earth.

Truly do not want to feel the pain of Earth *therefore, I am feeling the pain; pangs of Death, those who must die; are going to die.*

Listen, my battle here on Earth is not just physical but spiritual.

I see into the realm of Death, can see the faces of those who are on the Docket of Death, and it is painful.

Some who have died find me in the living.
Some speak to me.
Some want me to save them.

Therefore, I see and know. Know more than you think.

So yes, I have to hold on to God for grace; more than a saving grace.

There's a lot of evil here on Earth thus, **_Earth is the domain of Physical Death, and not Spiritual Death._**

Michelle

Oh God and Lovey, give me strength to go on; move forward truthfully on this day now, and forever ever without end.

LORD GIVE ME STRENGTH by the reggae artist Luciano.

Lovey, I am burdened by Death.
My body is so heavy that at times I cannot function; go on.
Life feel cursed to the amount of death that surrounds me.
The amount of death I see before it happens.
The dangers I see in life.

Visions – dreams and waking state visions of death is truly too much for me at times. I cannot go on at times. Please Lovey do not let me go mad; insane to the things I see because it's truly hard for me.

I walk alone.
Write alone.
Talk alone.
Is in this alone.

I need your strength Lovey because, I truly have none on my own.

Yes, at times I want to leave you, but you will not let me. By me leaving is suicide on my part, and path.

Dreams, some I do not want to talk about, but I have to I guess. Did not want to put the John Cena dream in this book, but the dream has been gnawing at me.

Dreamt John Cena and his teeth; him showing darkness in his mouth. I did not want to see John Cena in the dream, so I closed off the dream no wanting to go further with him.

I truly do not know Lovey, but my spirit cannot stand this guy in real life, and I truly do not know him.

There is something fake about him; gross.

No, I will not analyze this dream. Truly do not want to because Death must walk and take in the physical literally. You and I know this Lovey, so I am literally going to leave this dream alone. Refuse to analyze it. It's John Cena Lovey come on now.

Lovey, it's June 15, 2020.

THE SPIRITUAL

What is going on in the United States of America? Oh God Lovey this dream I had not too long ago that is leaving me disgusted again with Black People; Black Americans.

Lovey, with all I know it's a fool that go on the Battlefield of Death to fight for, and with Death's Own.

Lovey, it's a fool that fight for justice for the unjust; their unjust and wicked own. You are not true when you do this, you are just condoning the wrongs of those you fight for, and I've told you Lovey, I would never ever go on the Battlefield of Death to fight for Death's Own; Wicked and Evil Own. I refuse to.

My job is not Death's People but the good and true seed you've given me Lovey therefore, I complain to you when it comes to Death, and their wicked and evil own. I will not save anyone wicked and evil, nor will I go into any land and protest the evils of any politician for their people. Like I said, I complain to you. Therefore, I have let you Lovey be my news, and complaint outlet.

I cannot take humans therefore, I have to make you my fight, and true Love Lovey; with fight being my complaint outlet of goodness and truth; all that affect me here on Earth, in the Spiritual Realm, the Universe, and Beyond.

I have to make you my hope but with what I am seeing via my dream world, I need you to truly hear me, and listen to me truthfully, *and WALK AWAY FROM EVERY BLACK AMERICAN GLOBALLY. Allelujah*

ALL WHO FALL UNDER THE AMERICAN BANNER OF DEATH NO MATTER THE LAND, YOU MUST TRULY WALK AWAY FROM. *It is not wise Lovey for you to be amongst evil, side with evil, leave your life in the lands of evil amongst Death's True Own.*

You must get out of the lands of Death literally.
You can no longer protect and bless our enemies.
You can no longer let the lands, and people of Death benefit from life.

You need to uphold the law and laws of life therefore, it's time to walk away from death, the Lands and People of Death. You have to preserve the Lands and People of our good and true own only.

This morning I dreamt 3 flags.

The American Flag
The Jamaican Flag

I believe the third flag was the Brazilian Flag. I cannot fully remember because the American Flag, and Jamaican Flag was my concern.

The American Flag had no stars in it. See, in the dream *America waged war with Jamaica*, and that made me livid to the point of beyond anger. I asked in the dream, why would America wage war with Jamaica?

In the dream, the wind was blowing the American Flag; all three flags, but you saw the wind blowing the American Flag more.

After me being angry at America. I dreamt the now President of the United States Donald Trump.

You did not see him for long but briefly – but not in the way you can explain it. *He was there in the dream but was not.* I cannot explain it for humans to comprehend hence, I will leave things as is because; my Spiritual World do not flow like people think it should.

SO, WITH ME SEEING DONALD TRUMP BRIEFLY, BARRACK OBAMA WAS WITH HIM; SIDED AND OR, AGREED WITH HIM ON SOMETHING. WITH HIM BARRACK OBAMA AGREEING WITH AND OR, SIDING WITH DONALD TRUMP ALL YOU SAW WAS SOMEONE FIRING A GUN. THE BULLET CONNECTED IN BARRACK OBAMA'S HEAD, AND YOU COULD SEE; WELL I COULD SEE THE BULLET HOLE OF BLACK IN THE MIDDLE OF HIS HEAD.

They assassinated him Barrack Obama. What made things disheartening for me, it was Black Men in Gray that looked as if they had no soul that assassinated Barrack Obama in the dream.

When they assassinated Barrack Obama you saw the Secret Service firing shots killing some of the men that assassinated Barrack Obama.

The head guy of the Secret Service was a short Black Man, light skinned, and he reminded me of this actor; American Actor. I can see his face but cannot remember his name. No, it's not Clifton Davis but I believe he did some shows with Clifton Davis back in the day.

Those that did not die due to the Secret Service killing them were captured, and this light skinned Black Man went up to the one that survived and said something to him. I can't remember if he said, did you think I would not catch you? The captured, I can't remember if he said something. But the light skinned Black Man took a knife and slit the throat of the captured.

See all the men that killed Barrack Obama were Black.

After that you saw White People, with a different look on their face walking – not many White People walking. About 1 – 2 White People; male and female. I distinctly remember one older looking White Man in his fifties if not early sixties passing this huge stone – bolder. **_It was as if they did not care if Barrack Obama got assassinated._**

I do not know if they – he was lost. White People

After seeing that – the 1 – 2 White People walking, I was in this church. High up looking down, and White People were congregating. When I tell you congregating, I mean congregating to how full the church became of all White People. The preacher was singing and this White Lady that was beside me began to sing. Trust me she sang beautifully. So beautiful that the preacher invited her to sing, and sing she did about her hardship; no one knowing how hard her life was.

In the dream to me, she was seeking attention for her singing, and she got the attention.

After seeing that I believe the news got hold of the assassination of Barrack Obama and broadcasted it.

Now I was back in this house. The light skinned Black Man was now in the house. He was talking. I cannot tell you who the people looked like that he was talking to. See with the assassination of Barrack Obama they began to tarnish Barrack's name. His secretary – White Secretary came into play. They used her to tarnish his image by saying he Barrack Obama was having an affair with her. In the dream she dressed in Harlot's Clothing. **_(BC came to mind with his secretarial scandal.)_**

Purple Clothing that looked like chained clothing. She was on her hands and knees, and you could see her butt outlined in her Harlot Clothing.

In the dream, you did not see Michelle Obama. Then I thought about Barrack's children and how confused they were. In the dream, **_I could see the darkness of confusion around them – one of Barrack's daughter._**

Now after seeing all this, it was as if someone wanted to put up a huge picture of Ronald Reagan in the White House.

I did not see a picture of Ronald Reagan going up. I was now with the light skinned Black Man that killed Barrack Obama's assassins. I was telling him that I saw the Death of Barrack Obama long ago. He did not believe me, and tried to escape from me but fell down to the floor, and was crawling on the floor to get away from me. He did not want to hear what I had to say. **_I tried to tell him about RISE GOES UP_** – in this book I talked about Barrack Obama.

I can't remember if it was in *Book One of RISE GOES UP* I wrote about Barrack Obama and or, *Book Two*.

I don't know but I truly know.

After seeing all that via my dream world, I woke up, washed my face, and brushed my teeth. Looking at my face after washing it, there was blood in the middle of my forehead. My third eye indicator bled. I do not know why I am putting emphasis at seeing blood in my forehead. But somehow this blood to me has and have significance.

So, God is showing me things again. Now it's time for me to BLAST BLACK PEOPLE; THOSE BLACK SELL OUT AMERICANS THAT SELL OUT THEIR OWN – KILL THEIR OWN THEN CRY WOLF.

I truly do not care if Black Americans hate me. BUT BLACK AMERICANS ARE THE DEVIL'S OWN. BLACK DEVILS THAT ARE TRULY LOYAL TO WHITE DEATH.

Thus, they March, Protest, become Violent, Loot in their LYING GAME OF INJUSTICE. Therefore, no American will like Jamaicans because some of us see the evils of them as well as, the evils of Jamaicans – the Global Network of Evil.

IT IS BLACK AMERICANS THAT KILL THEIR OWN.
IT IS BLACK AMERICANS THAT SET UP THEIR OWN.

IT IS BLACK AMERICANS THAT HAS AND HAVE SACRIFICED SELF TO DEATH, AND THE PARTIES – SOCIETIES OF DEATH FOR A PAY CHEQUE THEN LIE ABOUT IT. LIE ABOUT SACRIFICING THEIR BROTHERS AND SISTERS – CASTING LOTS TO SEE WHICH ONE IN THE BLACK CIRCLE OF DEATH DIES NEXT.

Therefore Lovey, I would never ever go on the Battlefield of Death and fight for anyone Black based on hue, kinky hair, hue and evil deeds, and more.

I know Death.

Know Black Death, and I refuse to sacrifice myself to Death for anyone. It's a foolish person who go on the Battlefield of Death to fight for Death's Children and People. And, I refuse to be that foolish one. Thus, I will forever ever advocate for you Lovey to leave the Sell Out Blacks Globally behind. I cannot fight for them. *I refuse to because at the end of the day, MANY BLACKS – BILLIONS ARE LOYAL TO DEATH LITERALLY.*

So yes, <u>**MANY IN BLACK SOCIETY IS MENTALLY DISTURBED; DISEASED.**</u>

Many Blacks have sold their soul for riches; fame.

As you can see, **<u>many set you up, kill you.</u>** Therefore, I will forever say, it's a fool that fight for the devils own. People who have absolutely no value in life, or to life.

What we as Blacks fail to realize is that; <u>THERE ARE BLACK DEVILS OUT THERE THAT RIDE OFF THE COATTAIL OF BLACK PEOPLE.</u>

BLACK DEVILS WHOSE JOB IS TO CREATE STRIFE IN THE BLACK COMMUNITY BECAUSE IT IS GOOD; WISE FOR THEM. NO, PROFITABLE FOR THEM TO SEE BLACKS KILLING EACH OTHER, BLACKS LIVING IN DYSFUNCTION, BLACKS LIVING OFF THE SYSTEM AND SYSTEMS OF DEATH, BLACKS BEGGING BREAD, BLACKS LIVING IN SIN, BLACKS LIVING IN THE STREETS; HOMELESS, AND MORE.

<u>*So Lovey, you truly have to do something. You have to truly walk away from Black Americans because they are truly not apart of the True Black Race.* THEY BLACK AMERICANS CONTINUALLY MASSACRE THEIR OWN THEN TURN AROUND AND CRY WOLF FOR THE WORLD TO HAVE SYMPATHY ON THEM.</u>

<u>SO YES, I SEE AND KNOW WHY MOTHER AFRICA HAD TO EVICT SOME OF HER WICKED AND EVIL OWN.</u>

SHE GOT RID OF THEM. DID NOT WANT THEM IN HER. THEREFORE, THOSE BLACKS SHE GOT RID OF COULD NOT TO RETURN. SHE DID TURN FROM THEM BECAUSE SHE COULD NOT TAKE ANYMORE EVIL IN HER, AND THOSE LYING AFRICANS REFUSE TO TELL THE TRUTH OF SLAVERY, WHY MOTHER AFRICA EVICTED SOME OF HER EVIL OWN.

We still see this evil today. Because when you Lovey send people to help us in the West; many set up their own. But, I know Lovey that you will never ever let evil kill your good and true own.

So yes, Blacks are hypocrites because we do do all to discredit, and kill our Black Own. We continually cry for help, and when we get help, we spit in your face Lovey. So, I am truly telling you Lovey **<u>to walk away from the BLACK WOLVES IN SHEEP CLOTHING.</u>** *We do not need them, nor can we* AS TRUE BLACKS CARRY THE

BURDEN AND BURDENS OF THOSE LYING, AND DECEIVING BLACKS THAT DO ALL TO DISCREDIT, AND KILL THEIR BLACK OWN FOR A PLACE IN HELL WITH DEATH.

You cannot condone Black Sell Outs Lovey come on now.

As for my dream with Barrack Obama, I will not fully analyze this dream because Death must run to Death – the Houses of Death – Churches for a saving grace. (Cover up of the truth.) Thus, Death requires someone to be assassinated – sacrificed. Who is the question in the global political world; arena.

Black Jesus, and I will not go further with Black Jesus. I know who Black Jesus is given the story of Jesus as written in their; man's so-called holy bible. <u>But we know the full and true truth Lovey hence, I told you who Black Jesus is in RISE GOES UP. Black sacrifice.</u>

So yes, I am fed up of People hence, Black People need to get their ass whooped for the lies they accept, preach, teach, and more. I will not, <u>refuse to BLAME YOU LOVEY FROM WALKING AWAY FROM BLACK PEOPLE GLOBALLY BECAUSE WI TOO FOOL FOOL.</u>

<u>DON'T BLAME LIFE</u> by the reggae artist Bugle.

We have life.

Can write our good and true life with God; Lovey but, we refuse to acknowledge life.

We continually accept the lies of the different nations then complain to Lovey; God about how the different races are evil towards us.

We are the ones to cause our hurt and pain.
We are the ones that like to live mentally insane.
Live in dysfunctional lifestyles.
Make our life dysfunctional.
Believe, and accept the lies of other nations.

We refuse to build our own true nations based on true unity, true Black Life.

We refuse good counsel. So, why should God continually hear haade eaase people?

People that truly do not want or need to build them self and the community you live in positively. Blacks globally are truly not growing truthfully, or positively, and we are not seeing this.

<u>*CHANGE YOUR LIFE*</u> *by the reggae artist Bushman.*

<u>*LUCIANO MEETS BUSHMAN REGGAE ROOTS AND CULTURE MIXTAPE by Djeasy Mixmaster.*</u>

It is us as Black People who refuse to change our Life.
It is us as Black People that hear but truly do not listen.

It is us as Black People that read without reading with comprehension, cannot decipher what we read. Thus, we lack true knowledge.

Some are so blind that they cannot see the confusion and lies before them. See your so-called holy bible that depict God as a monster that at times you have to wonder why God still try with man - humans. <u>Therefore, a RACE AND PEOPLE THAT KNOWETH NOT LIFE CANNOT TEACH YOU THE TRUTH, AND TRUE TRUTH OF GOD. GOD IS CLEAN NOT DIRTY.</u>

Onwards I go.

Some of you refuse to know that; <u>when you bow down to the ground and pray, GOD IS AGAINST YOU. LITERALLY WALK AWAY FROM YOU.</u>

BOWING DOWN TO THE GROUND IS A LITERAL SIN. YOU ARE CURSING YOURSELF AS A PERSON, AND YOU ARE CURSING THE LAND; GROUND YOU BOW DOWN TO.

GOD IS UP NOT DOWN.
So, pray sitting up
Standing up
Or, laying upright in your bed.

DEATH IS DOWN.
ALL THAT IS FILTHY IS DOWN.
YOU PUT; BURY YOUR DEAD DOWN.
YOU PUT YOUR GARBAGE DOWN.
YOU PUT THE FILTH YOU PASS OUT OF YOUR BODY DOWN.

THEREFORE, GOD CANNOT BE DOWN. GOD MUST BE UP BECAUSE GOD IS CLEAN; NOT FILTHY.

WHEN YOU BOW DOWN TO THE GROUND, YOU ARE TELLING GOD YOU ARE PRAYING TO THE FILTH OF THE EARTH. YOU TRULY DO NOT WANT, OR NEED GOOD AND TRUE LIFE.

Therefore, when the righteous take up for the wicked and evil, they are condoning the wrongs of evil. You cannot look down to God, you have to; must look up.

No one can look to evil – evil people for salvation come on now. Therefore; you Lovey cannot take up for a race and people; the Black Race that continually sell out their own, for the wrongs; nastiness of the different races then cry racism; foul.

You Lovey cannot continue to tolerate and look the other way when it comes to Blacks Globally. Meaning, you cannot save people that truly refuse to change their dirty linen of clothing. You've been trying for centuries, and still the Black Race have not learned; refuse to change their dirty linen of self. They continue to think their wrongs will save them.

You Lovey is/are trying in vain for people who refuse the truth. Time and time again you've shown me that Blacks will refuse me, this is true because many cannot see their life, and hell before them. Instead we accept lies – lies that break us up into tribes – different classes – nations. Thus, causing us to lose our life and way.

Many refuse to let go of the occult – different religious lies we've been indoctrinated in. Religious lies that has and have chained; locked many in hell literally.

Look at the different organizations of Death; religious groups in Islam, and Christianity that many Blacks are affiliated with. Cults that teach violence, hate, incest, dysfunctional living, different forms of fornication, and more. These people Lovey you cannot see with or want. Religion paint you so filthy that I have to wonder about you including, doubt you.

When did you Lovey become the cesspool; hog for human thought, living, learning, teachings, culture, life, religions, and more?

<u>TRUE LIFE IS HONEST, CLEAN, EASY TO LIVE, EVER GROWING UP GOOD AND TRUE, CANNOT DIE</u>, therefore, you are being cautioned by me Lovey. Please do not be angry at me, but you cannot look at Black Americans and want to save them. These Blacks are a different breed of Blacks and you know this. You know how wicked and evil these Blacks are therefore, you cannot have any mercy for them, nor have a place with you, or in you for them; Americans.

They are truly happy regressive niggers that cannot learn, and see their own destruction. Therefore, you cannot see with them Black Americans Globally.

True change come from within.

YOU CANNOT FIGHT TO LIVE IN REGRESSIVE SOCIETIES.

You cannot fight for change in systems that are not yours; was never yours.

Stop fighting, and start building you truthfully.

You cannot want, need, and fight people for what's not yours. You are a liar and dyam red yie when you do this. Therefore, you are no different from those who abuse you.

Therefore Lovey, they, (Black Americans) are truly not of us; the True Black Race.

<u>You cannot want truth for Blacks without knowing the full and true truth of self, your past, your true roots of then and now.</u>

Therefore Lovey, the truth; full truth about Jesus must be told. I have to complete this book.

<u>I refuse to sit and watch Black Demons kill their own.</u> It's happened way to often over the years and centuries. I will never forget what Black Americans did to Marcus Mosiah Garvey. Nor will I forget what Jamaicans did to him; Marcus Mosiah Garvey, and other Black Freedom Fighters before him.

Unlike these Freedom Fighters Lovey, I refuse to petition you for all Blacks. I truly refuse to, and even if you Lovey were to say; Michelle save all Blacks, I would turn my back on you, and truly go against you because; you would have been evil; wicked and evil to me, and self. <u>I know how evil many BLACKS ARE TO THEIR OWN.</u>

I know how wicked and evil we (Blacks) are to self, and each other. Therefore, many in the Black Community Globally use evil; negative forces to carry down, kill, harm, tun dung, set duppy pan others, teef peeple man an oman, sprinkle powda a peeple yaade, and more. So no, I truly cannot pray for the wicked, and evil of the Black Race.

Yes, I am disturbed by the dream (Barrack Obama dream) above but, I cannot let this dream fully disturb me. I know the evils of the Black Race.

<u>Our enemies use many in the Black Race to do their dirty bidding</u> and, instead of us as Blacks uniting truthfully and say; I am out of these corrupt and dysfunctional societies, we stay in them.

Fight, march, protest to stay in them – dysfunctional societies globally.

Look at me Lovey, I need to be out of the environment I am in. And, no matter how I pray to you for a true and peaceful place; environment where I am truly happy in, you ignore me, but the Black Devils of the Globe you see with truthfully.

So now tell me Lovey, if you are not truly willing to change your dirty ways, how can I change mine?

How can anyone change their dirty linen of self?

Are we not failing then?
Are we not failures with you, and in you?

Can anyone live in lies and expect to find truth?

Are lies not lies?

So, how can you Lovey leave those who are of life in unclean, and dysfunctional societies globally?

When we live amongst and with dysfunctional people, do we not become dysfunctional like them; the dysfunctional?

Including, unclean, and dysfunctional families globally.

Are you Lovey not saying you are dysfunctional also?

You Lovey need to truly think. You cannot let the captives; evils, and evil people of the Physical Realm, Spiritual Realm, the Universe, and Beyond continue to go free. You cannot continue to condone the wicked and evil ways of humans no matter the colour, race, creed, culture, heritage, descent, and more come on now.

Freedom is a must because the good and true need their freedom, and all you Lovey are telling me is that you truly don't give a damn.

The time of evil is up. I did not choose wicked and evil for myself, my family, you, my gorgeous and beautiful mother, the good and true seeds you've given me, the moon, and more, so why are you failing me Lovey?

Why are you not truly listening to me, and heeding my goodness for us and our good and true own only?

Unless, your good and true own is Death's Children and People?

Yes, you can be pissed at me, but you too Lovey need to CHANGE YOUR LIFE, AND LIFESTYLE.

You cannot say you are clean and leave our good and true own amongst the unclean.

Earth is like unto Sodom and Gomorrah I know this.

Humans did make Earth the Paradise of Death; Physical Death.

I need to move on without Death. My body cannot take anymore. I know it is going to get worse on Earth because, *DEATH'S CHILDREN AND PEOPLE MUST FULFILL DEATH'S PROPHECY.*

They, Death's Children, and People must; have to make Earth a Death Zone where people live to kill for want of food, clean drinking water, medication, and more.

You Lovey cannot say you are of life; the true and living God, and lead us blindly; cause us to die.

This; Death is all good for those who fall under the White Banner of Death, but all in all Lovey, *we have to save our good and true own only.*

We have to prepare a place for our good and true own.

WORRIES AND PROBLEM by *Bushman the reggae artist.*

How much more should some sing about the corrupt of Black Society?

How much more songs must go up to you Lovey for you to hear; listen, and do something constructive and true to shut the wicked and evil of Earth, the Spiritual Realm, the Universe, and Beyond down?

All I see Lovey is. Billions here on Earth is/are your true enemies that care not for life – You.

Lovey, if you leave people in poverty, they will do illegal things to get by. I know all is truly not lost, and yes, I know the fight within our Black Communities Globally.

Some Blacks we need to let go of yes, I know. Therefore, I have to come to you Lovey and not man.

Now Lovey tell me this.

Why should the 1% of the globe own it all whilst leaving billions begging for bread?

Now let me ask you Lovey.
Was this Covid-19 pandemic called for?

How many has and have lost their jobs?
How many have truly died?

How much/many more will be evicted from their homes – become homeless?

Why is life a game, and act for the White Race?
Do they not know there is no life for them?

There is a hell Lovey yet, humans do not think of their Spiritual Hell. The pain they have to – must face in their hell.

Lovey with this pandemic, how much more should live on the streets while the 1% gain financially?

The net worth of the 1% has and have increased substantially while the poor, and in need are losing it all.

Yes, I know you've truly provided for me during this Covid-19 pandemic, and I have to truly thank you for supporting me, and preserving me. But Lovey, we need a true and just society globally for our good and true own only.

Water is getting scarce. I see this and know this. Therefore, I have to secure my home with clean drinking water.

Michelle

JAH LIVE RIDDIM 2008 released by Joe Frasier

It's June 16, 2020 and wow to my night. My shoulder pain would not release me from it – the pain in my body.

It's morning now and I have to give God; Lovey thanks for letting me make it through my Hell of Pain.

Now I am listening to the Jah Live Riddim with Taurus Riley, Etana, Mikey Spice, Duane Stephenson, and Luciano. Needed to listen to this riddim this morning because I needed these songs.

These songs are songs of vision, hope, and more to what's going on globally with this man-made Pandemic. Covid-19

See right now while Blacks in the United States carry out their job of looting and rioting, marching, and making a fool of themselves when it comes to systems put in place to deceive them, due to so called American Systemic Racism, the globe is truly not seeing what is going on behind closed doors.

Right now, businesses are being closed down therefore, income is being lost for many.

More self-check-out machines are being installed in stores, therefore; income is being lost for many.

(ONE WORLD ORDER, CURRENCY, GLOBAL SLAVERY, DEATH TRAP GLOBALLY)

Food shortage is going to come into play – and you know what, I already talked about this in other books. ***Further, the great Robert Nesta Marley aka, Bob Marley told us this decades ago in AMBUSH IN THE NIGHT.***

Marcus Mosiah Garvey tried to educate us as Blacks about enterprise, thinking wise, doing wise things, going back to Africa, Black Economics and more, and we as Blacks set him up. DID ALL TO BETRAY HIM, AND DID BETRAY HIM.

GOD did all to help us by sending different people throughout the ages and centuries to help us to get back to life and as BLACKS, MANY JOINED WITH DEATH TO BETRAY LIFE; GOD BY CONTINUING TO TAKE OUR LIFE FROM LIFE. See religion and politics, and the different religions, and political wars throughout the ages; centuries including now with the different lands globally.

We as Blacks are so stupid that we cannot see what's going on around us.

We fight amongst ourselves thus, giving the Devil the victory over us literally.

See Black on Black crimes that keep us ignorant – stupid because we continually defend all that is wrong. Therefore, Blacks are the ones committing Suicide Globally without knowing it. **_LOVE CREATED I_ by Tarrus Riley.**

So as Blacks we've become true fools without roots that continually defend, and live wrong globally. Then expect people to pity us for the lies we accept, and live in.

So, I was thinking and talking to God yesterday about what's happening with this Pandemic in regards to; people wearing face masks everywhere they go.

I was thinking, and saying; with people wearing face mask everywhere they go, what is to stop people from using this – these masks – this benefit of wearing masks to go out there to rob, kill, rape, invade people's homes, and more?

Then this morning my dream world would not let up on me seeing White People including Racist, and Entitled Whites using their mask privilege to rob this gas station, and treating people like crap. This one White Man had the gaul to try to take me on, and I put him in his place in the dream.

No people, I am not having it when it comes to White People who feel the need to think they are better than everyone else. To me, **_this Inept Race need a lesson in life, and civility – truth._** *Look at the world globally to the way it is being run by them. Earth has been, and is a literal cesspool of sin and dismay since this race (the White Race) took power and, I truly do not know why God truly have them here on Earth amongst us.* Yes, racist but this morning I truly do not care. I see the havoc that is going to be unleashed here on Earth shortly to what must come – them fulfilling the WILL OF THEIR GOD – DEATH. Their final war.

Life have no worth to this race thus, they deceive at will, kill at will, destroy at will, lie at will, blame at will, and more evil things.

I see what's to come yet, *our STUPID, IGNORANT, INEPT BLACKS GLOBALLY CANNOT SEE BECAUSE THEY LET WHITES BLIND THEM WITH LIES.*

Feed them lies that they willingly gobble up. Therefore, Blacks will forever be the White Man's Guinea Pigs literally.

Thus, you do have DEMONIC BLACKS – BLACK DEVILS THAT SIDE, AND WILL FOREVER SIDE WITH DEATH TO DESTROY BLACK LIVES; THEIR BLACK OWN.

THE SPIRITUAL

Blacks are used as scapegoats and guinea pigs globally, and many in the Black Community Globally are at fault for this.

Many think everything White is good.

Well, what about everything Black that is good?
What about our true Black Roots with God; Life?
What about our true place with God?

<u>Why lose it for Fools Gold that have absolutely no worth in Life, or with God?</u>

Therefore, none in the Black Race can tell me anything. All I have to do is GO TO GOD FOR WHOM I CALL LOVEY FROM TIME TO TIME.

Things God/Lovey reveal to me truthfully. Therefore, I see the crap of dung that will be unleashed on humans globally and them; humans not seeing their life in front of them. I see the hell of some. Lord have mercy.

We are being controlled, and will be further controlled. Well you and not me because, God/Lovey is my good and true pilot; navigator in life. Therefore, if I can write the evils of all out of Life, the Physical Realm, Spiritual Realm, the Universe, Beyond the Universe, in the hearts of every human I would without hesitation and Lovey truly know this. I truly do not need evil in my life; good and true life, or around me.

I need true peace.
True love.
True, good, and positive growth.
True, good, and positive building.

True, good, truly peaceful, truly positive living here on Earth, and everywhere good and true life resides including here on Earth.

As Blacks we cannot continue to open up our Garden of Eden to negative; evil people of the different races, and culture.

Like I've said in other books including this one. God did try to help us, Black People. *<u>It is us as BLACKS THAT CONTINUALLY FAIL SELF, AND GOD.</u>*

<u>Blacks are failures to self and life therefore, BLACK LIVES MATTER TO THOSE WHO DESTROY US; DO ALL TO KILL US DUE TO THE LIES WE ACCEPT ABOUT OUR SELF, OUR ANCESTRY, ROOTS, CULTURE, LIES WE LIVE BY, TEACH OUR CHILDREN, AND BY TEACHING OUR CHILDREN</u>

THESE LIES WE'VE ACCEPTED, WE'VE PASSED THESE LIES UNTO OUR CHILDREN; FUTURE GENERATIONS TO LITERALLY DIE BY.

Life is truly easy, it's us as BLACKS THAT CONTINUALLY FORCE OURSELVES TO GO INTO LANDS; PLACES THAT TRULY DO NOT LIKE US; DON'T WANT US THERE.

INSTEAD OF TRULY BUILDING US, WE BUILD THE ECONOMY OF OTHERS, THEN CRY ABOUT THE NEGATIVE TREATMENT WE GET.

So no, I refuse to GO ON THE BLACK LIVES MATTER TRAIN BECAUSE IT IS US AS BLACKS THAT DERAIL US.

How many have and has marched and lost their lives when it comes to Blacks, and the injustice they face globally?

BLACK INJUSTICE TRULY TO DO NOT HAVE TO BE. BUT AS FOOLS WE BUILD OTHERS INSTEAD OF BUILDING OUR SELF POSITIVELY, AND ECONOMICALLY. INSTEAD OF BUILDING US WISE – POSITIVE, WE TEAR DOWN EACH OTHER.

TEAR DOWN OUR COMMUNITY.
TEAR DOWN OUR LIFE.
EVEN TEAR DOWN GOD.

So no, I refuse to stand with LIARS AND THIEVES THAT KNOW NOT WHO THEY ARE, WHERE THEY STAND IN LIFE WITH SELF AND GOD, WHERE THEY CAME FROM, HAVE NO ROOTS BECAUSE, THEY DID NOT WATER THEIR TREE OF LIFE WITH GOD. THEY MADE THEIR TREE STARVE, ROT, AND DIE.

Blacks are liars and thieves therefore, the dysfunctional state we live in, breathe in, die in.

LEARN TO LOVE by Etana.

It's time we as Blacks learn the truth of self.
Our generational past.
Our true roots with God.
Our true creation.

Our life in life, and more.

It's only when we can respect self, we can respect others including God.

Yes, there's more that I want to say in regards to what is to come, and the assassination of Barrack Obama in the dream above but, I refuse to; cannot. **_I NEED BLACKS TO FIGURE OUT THE DREAM._**

Yes, when it comes to sacrifices because; many Blacks in America – the United States of America no matter the social and or, economic class is/are sacrificed.

*Many are passed around like handouts for those who own them. Therefore, in true reality, **BLACKS ARE STILL BOUGHT AND SOLD LITERALLY.***

Did I dream Russia a few days ago?

Yes, thus my favorite Russian had no smile on his face. **_It was as if DARKNESS FELL OVER RUSSIA._**

So not going to analyze this dream either. Like I said, I know what is to happen to Humans, and this Earth Globally shortly.

Truly not going to worry about the people of this Earth. All must come to an halt for the wicked and evil, therefore, humans are the ones to kill each other due to foolishness like race, religion, sex, politics, generational curse, people using evil to influence others, the lies humans tell each other, deceit, and more evil things.

I cannot be mindful of people especially those in the Black Race who truly disgrace Black Life. Are wolves in sheep clothing.

I cannot pretend to be Black. I know I am Black, therefore; I have sight to see into the different lands except for China. When it comes to China, I am being blocked big time from seeing the happenings of this land.

When I look at this Covid-19 Pandemic and see the fraudulent nature of it. I think of the future and how the different governments are creating a system where looting, more killing is going to be on Earth. There's enough crazy people out there, and with shortage of food, people are going to get crazier, and more people are going to die. Plus, their deathtology/deathnology is being implanted more and more.

Humans' aren't seeing this but I am.

Just this morning June 17, 2020, I dreamt John Cena and Dwayne "The Rock" Johnson. They were somewhere and both men had a coconut for which they drank the water. After they drank the water, the coconut became heavy for them. They could not lift it, and at one point the coconut became so large about 10 times the average size of a water coconut without the ux – outer shell. The large coconut dropped on John Cena's head, and he tried to get it off for which he did.

Seeing all this, I went to lift up the coconut and chopped it with a machete. In the dream I said, this they could not lift. The coconut was light for me, but heavy for the men.

Chopping the coconut, it was not good inside, and you could see this brown thing in the coconut. Continuing to chop, some parts of the coconut looked as if it had oil in it – ready to make oil. I showed the men the bad areas of the coconut.

Oh man, I am missing a part of the dream where John Cena, and The Rock; Dwayne Johnson was hugging, and the Rock; Dwayne Johnson who was now dressed in Hawaiian attire began to cry. Then he let go of John Cena, and sat down beside him; John Cena.

Then I was showing them the coconut; inside of the coconut that they drank. After that the army came. This guy that sounded British was not happy about the army that came. He, and his men to him should have been the first to go into this cave. Cave is how I can describe it.

Do I truly want to analyze this dream?

No

Truly do not care for The Rock "Dwayne Johnson," and John Cena. However, I am thinking about Samoa, and Hawaii; the coconut trees of those lands, and what is going to happen to them for them to go bad. Or, if some disaster is going to hit these lands.

Yes, I know we are in a time of Germ, and Chemical Warfare. I know there are chemicals out there that can literally kill the coconut trees of any given land. So yes, more is going to happen globally to the food supply and or, food chain of man.

You have sick people out there that are cold hearted. THEY TRULY DO NOT CARE WHO THEY HURT, AND KILL. Death is their game, and they will, and do kill at will.

So no, the future of humans is truly not bright given the state, and states of confusion the different governments, and mega corporations of the globe put us in. Therefore, the different roles of the Mafia - Governments, and Corporations of the Globe play with the life of people; humans.

Not one of us can BLAME GOD FOR THE STATE HUMANS ARE IN.

God didn't have our children for us.
God didn't elect demons to oversee any of us.
God most certainly did not give anyone unjust, and unfair laws to live and die by.

God most certainly did not give anyone unjust, and unfair laws to give to anyone globally.

God did not create the mess on/in Earth, we as people; individuals did.

God did not create weapons and give to anyone to kill others by.

God did not take life from anyone here on Earth. It is us as humans that take our life from God due to sin, the people we elect to govern us, the corporations we support that deceive us, even kill us. See the different chemicals, viruses, nuclear weapons, guns, ammunitions, war machines, diseases and more that man create to destroy, and kill.

I truly do not know why lies have to be the focal point in human life with the different races. The reason being is my dream this morning June 19, 2020 where I dreamt people being paid to protest Justin Trudeau.

How stupid can people be? You vote people into office and when they do not live up to your expectations you do shit to slander them, protest against them, destroy statues you've erected, some even protest the statues of their slave masters.

I refuse racism and the racial bullshit of this world, but I refuse to give into bully tactics of any race. There is something called freedom of expression; speech, and if this is how I feel it is how I feel. <u>Don't like it, don't live in my country.</u> Stay the bleep out.

Hence, I am a true separatist.

These books; you don't like them, don't read them straight up. They are not for you. As long as I am not spreading hate or hurting you, I am truly good to go, but I refuse to change me to please you or anyone. I've learnt the hard way that you cannot please people, you have to please yourself, and live right with God.

If you've elected people that do not have your best interest at heart, truly blame you and not the person you elect. You did not respect yourself to elect good governance for self.

Talk is cheap thus, you have many truly cheap monsters; politicians out there. *I am also dreaming about God, and I truly cannot tell you which land God is against right now. I truly cannot remember the dream. God did walk away from a race; I am not sure if it's the White Race again, but for you in the White Race based on physical hue, and spiritual hue, truly good luck because the worst is yet to come for you.*

One by one God is walking away from people. So, truly good luck to humans here on Earth. Many think God is with them, but God is truly not with you. I know this for a fact without doubt.

We cannot do all the evils here on Earth and think God is going to stay with us. God is not going to stay with us hence, I told you in another book. We are in the days of **Malachi.** I refuse to read Malachi hence my disobedience. Maybe one day I will read it, but for now I am leaving man's so-called holy books of lies alone.

Humans live by lies.
Religious lies.
Scientific lies.
Medical lies.
Psychological lies.
Economic lies.
Family lies.
Generational lies.
Biblical lies – Mythology
Political lies.

Historical lies, and more, and I am tired of it. Meaning, <u>tired of us expecting God to save us from the lies we accept, and believe in.</u>

If you have not truth, you cannot be saved because all you have are lies. You live in lies, and believe in lies. This is why God have to walk away from billions.

We cannot talk about God without speaking the truth and addressing the truth. When I see my own Black People, I am disgruntled because; <u>WE CONTRIBUTE TO OUR OWN DOWNFALL.</u>

Blacks do not have to live the way we do, but you have some in the Black Community that profit off the negative way we as Blacks are living therefore, contributing to the demise of the Black Race. <u>The beauty of land is truly not the beauty of people; those who live in that land. Therefore, humans make the land they live in, and the lands of others ugly and desolate as them. Africa, Jamaica, all the Caribbean.</u>

It is us as a race and people (Blacks) that refuse to acknowledge the fact that there are BLACK DEMONS AMONGST US. We paint this rosy picture of Black People being abused. Now tell me, <u>can a man fight for justice in systems that were designed by the unjust?</u>

Can the Black Race find justice in systems that were truly not meant for them?

If you know the systems of men; the White Man is unjust, why fight to stay in that unjust system?

Why not have your own systems of justice that is fair, and true; just?

<u>ABSOLUTELY NO ONE HAVE TO LIVE THE WHITE WAY – DEATH'S WAY.</u>

Globally Whites are not the dominant race. No, that's a lie. Some Blacks fall under the White Banner of Death thus, Earth is the Physical Domain of Death. Death's Children and People control Earth thus, the dysfunctional living of the different races, and people globally.

So yes, Death has a job to do, but **LIFE ALSO HAVE A JOB TO DO**.

Right now, Death's Children and People are secured in hell. There are no ands, ifs, or buts about this. Billions do have their name in the Book of Death already. And, for those who think.

Read this:

<u>It is now forbidden for anyone Black to save anyone in the White Race for saving sake.</u>

So, if you were banking on the BLACK BANK, AND BI-RACIAL BANK, those banks are now void; indefinitely closed.

Yes, your JESUS BANK is officially NULL, AND VOID.

Why should anyone Black Live, or Die to save the wicked and evil of this Earth; those who truly hate the Black Race, and use us as your; their experimental guinea pigs, scapegoats, and more? You sinned; you must be held accountable for your sins period. Therefore no one White can escape their hell, and rightfully so.

DEATH'S CHILDREN AND PEOPLE DID TEACH ALL OF HUMANITY HOW TO DIE. FROM THE LIES THEY TELL TO THE MOVIES YOU WATCH, THE WAY YOU LIVE YOUR LIFE, THE WAY YOU HATE EACH OTHER, KILL EACH OTHER, DIE AMONGST EACH OTHER, MARRY EACH OTHER, PROCREATE WITH EACH OTHER, AND MORE. This is your life of Sin not Good.

The job of Life – the Children and People of God is to teach those that belong to God how to maintain and sustain life so that when Final Death begin to take on a massive scale, God's Children and People are saved.

We as God's Children and People have to know how to live.
We have to know how to call on God for help.
We have to be living right – truthfully.
We have to segregate our self from Death's Children and People.
We truly have to learn how to live.

Right now, no one is living, not even me. No, I am living but I am not living the way I truly want and need to. I truly need to give, but right now, I cannot give due to this lock down, and my financial inability.

Yes, you can give prayer, but who do I give prayer to when I truly do not know people, nor is it everyone you can, or should pray for?

GOD IS NOT FOR EVERYONE. Therefore, it's not everyone you can go to God and pray for, this I know for a fact.

Jamaica is a testament for me and prayer; people who you are not to pray for because God did deem this land unclean. Therefore, the land is beautiful but the mind, and heart of the people are truly dirty; mucky.

THE SPIRITUAL

Many people talk about God without knowing; truly knowing who God is.

For many, God is the nasty creature in man's so-called holy book; bible.

Know this. *God keep the Children and People of Life out of unclean places,* so now tell me, how can God be that unclean creature; demon of man's so-called holy bible when God is truly clean, and not dirty?

Why do we paint God as a monster when monsters are humans?

Is it not humans that do the bidding of Death?
Is it not humans that live to die instead of living to live?

Is it not humans that have and has forgotten that there is life beyond the grave?

Is it not humans that have and has forgotten that when the spirit shed the flesh there is a life and death that must be had; faced for some?

Many speak about the spirit, but truly do not know about the spiritual.

I've told you in other books, life is not flesh alone. Our life is spirit also therefore, spiritual life, and spiritual death is not contained here on Earth. Not because you cannot see into the Spiritual Realm does not mean that life and death do not exist there.

I've also told you in other books. *The life you live here on Earth determines where you go once the spirit shed the flesh.*

So, when some say, Jesus is going to save them, I say truly good luck to you because, I know the truth of Jesus.

I know the truth of God, and I've told you in other books. *God would never ever let any of his or her Children and People die to save the wicked and Evil.* If God allowed and or, allow any Child, or Anyone of Life to die to save Death's Wicked and Evil Own then *God would have been a LIAR; A TRUE AGENT OF DEATH. Death's Bitch.*

Life cannot die to save Death because, <u>DEATH CANNOT BE SAVED.</u> DEATH CAN ONLY DIE THUS, THE HELL OF THOSE WHO CREATED HELL FOR SELF.

GOD CANNOT CREATE HELL FOR YOU BECAUSE, GOD KNOW NOT HELL.

GOD DID NOT CREATE HELL FOR YOU BECAUSE, GOD DID NOT SIN FOR YOU. YOU SINNED FOR SELF.

GOD CANNOT KNOW HELL BECAUSE, GOD IS CLEAN NOT DIRTY.

Yes, I see into hell. Can tell some of their hell but, this is because I am here on Earth. If I was not here on Earth, I would not be able to tell you of you. You wouldn't know me people, nor would I want to know the confines, and evils of Earth; you.

So yes, this is why God is elusive; cannot be found for some. Truth is not within billions therefore, Death is the God for some; well, billions.

To stray a bit.

You know what is so hypocritical about the people of this world. When all is calm Black History, Black Inventions, Black Life matter not. But when something goes wrong, you see the hypocrites <u>MARCHING ABOUT RACISM.</u> You do not see these hypocrites any other time. But as soon as Blacks start something – protesting, you see the hypocrites jumping on the Racism bandwagon as if they are truly with Black People, and the unfair treatment Blacks get globally by the different races.

Damn. Yes, I want to swear but I am going to leave things alone. I know shortly every White Person Globally must pay because this is truly not done. Hell must come down to Earth.

Allelujah

Woe because if any White Person Globally think God is with them, they had truly better think again.

Si hell dey! But then, WHITES TRULY DO NOT KNOW THAT THEY ARE HELL BOUND, <u>AND THE BLACK SAVIOUR THEY ARE LOOKING FOR TO SAVE THEM FROM HELL IS TRULY NO MORE LITERALLY.</u>

<u>Unfair systems beget unfair treatment of people; the masses.</u>

<u>CHANGE YOUR LIFE</u> by the reggae artist Bushman.

Black People we have to change our life if we want; need a better tomorrow.

Absolutely no one can change us apart from us. Therefore, <u>it is wise to leave behind those Blacks that tear us down behind closed doors then come around with their false talk saying; they are with us when they are truly not with us.</u>

Blacks must not rise for some. We must live as the dung of the Earth.
To repeat: <u>CHANGE YOUR LIFE</u> by the reggae artist Bushman.

<u>TRAVELER</u> by the reggae artist Luciano

It's time for true Blacks to return home and build Mother Africa truthfully without the lies we've been taught by those who truly hate us. So, they do all to deceive us as Blacks, taint our heritage, water down us as a people, and what we've done to civilize the uncivilized.

The uncivilized cannot be civilized, and we as Blacks need to know this.

Hogs will be hogs. Therefore, it is unwise to want to change people.

<u>TELL ME WHY</u> by the reggae artist Luciano

Trust me, ***I know the judgement of the White Race, and absolutely none can get away from their judgement.***

Wow to the hell of this race hence, I worry not about any because none have and has thought about HELL. Their punishment – Death Sentence.

<u>GET UP STAND UP</u> by Robert Nesta Marley aka, Bob Marley.

As Blacks we need to move away from the systems that oppress us; keep us down. By us as a race and people establishing our own economy that is self reliant; not dependent on the oppressive economies of others then we will be fine.

<u>It's time we have our own including have our own God. We have to get our God back. If we don't do this, we will never be better as a race and people.</u>

<u>When we get back to truth, we will become unstoppable because no one can touch us; God is truly with us.</u> We will not faulter because, we are holding on to God and more importantly, <u>we are listening to God.</u> For example, Pastor whatever come to you and say. My Brother, Black Brother my god is great. He gives you all. All you have to do is follow me, come to my church, mosque, home, park, outdoor setting and hear me; what my god say. Here let me leave you this book, or pamphlet. You smile and say, "no thank you."

He still stands there trying to convince you of his god. And you cry out and say; Lovey this what's it, what's it not fool is trying to convince me of his God, want me to turn from you. Truly remove him from my door. Better yet, truly do not let any demon come to my door to try and take me from you. I am of life not death, and Death's Children and People should not bother me with their nonsense of their God.

I truly do not need Death in my life. Thus, as Blacks we need to be satisfied, and not want what the next man has and or, have. Plus, when you know God, you cannot be rocked, or moved.

When you know God, you keep the Truth of God.

When you know God, evil do fear you because; you will be able to command Death.

God do stand with you. Therefore, <u>**KNOW GOD,**</u> and not believe.

The only way God leave out of your life, is if you let God go.

<u>**THERE'S A GREAT TRIBULATION COMING.**</u> As Blacks we truly need to prepare for this. *The different systems of the corrupt from then until now has, and have made sure that God cannot come into Earth.*

Made sure they took God from us.
Made sure we live in sin.

Live and die with sins that are numberless due to the cost; penalty of 1 sin.

They've made sure some of you rack up so much sin that you cannot be saved. Your name is taken out of the Book of Life, and put in the Book of Death literally.

Many; when your spirit shed the flesh, you automatically go to hell. So yes, in all the White Race has and have done, <u>***THEY HAVE SEALED THE FATE OF EVERY WHITE PERSON BASED ON HUE, INCLUDING SPIRITUAL HUE IN HELL.***</u>

See, everyone that has and have signed on the dotted line to fight, go to war; go against life have sinned – have and has automatically died. Your name cannot be retrieved from the Book of Death. There are no ands, ifs, or buts about this. This is your fate because you willingly, and knowingly went against Life; God. And yes, I've discussed this in other books.

So no, I cannot worry about what WHITE PEOPLE DO BECAUSE, I KNOW FOR A FACT. **_THEY HAVE NO PLACE WITH GOD ANYMORE. THE DAMAGE HAS, AND HAVE BEEN DONE._**

It is us as Black People that need to change our dirty ways, and prepare for the future – ensure our future generations have lands to live on – in. We cannot continually let the hogs – swines' we elect to oversee us continually sell off Black Lands to the highest bidder, and when time come; our young children – future generations of youths have absolutely nothing to call their own.

<u>Other nations that truly hate us, treat us poorly; unfairly, unjust, kill us, defame us, use us, abuse us should not be developing Black Nations, and profiting off us when we have Black People that can, and do need work. We need to positively invest in our future, and the future of our future generations. We need to build our Black Lands, People, and Industries truly POSITIVE; BLACK. We have to truly respect our True Black Being, and Culture; God.</u>

<u>We cannot leave our future generations with nothing so that they suffer like we've suffered.</u> We are wrong when we do this. Why want our future generations of innovators to become beggars, and thieves?

Africa is vast, but who is developing Africa?

The Caribbean is vast but who is developing the Caribbean?

If we do not set good values for our children today, how are they to grow good?
How are they to learn good?
How are they to develop good?

As Blacks we continually rape our future generations of their wealth, and then wonder why we as Blacks are so broke and destitute financially, health wise, mentally, spiritually, life wise, God wise, and more.

Look at it. Despite the lies, thievery, and murderous ways of the White Race based on hue, and evil deeds. <u>*They: Whites did secure their future.*</u> Yes, in an evil way, but they do control the Global Economy, and many Black Lands. *<u>They: Whites made sure they decimated; killed Black Civilization, Black History, Black Life, Black Culture, and more importantly, OUR BLACK GOD.</u>*

So, if we do not secure the future of Blacks – our future generations now, our children – future generations will have nothing.

<u>Right now, we have nothing because Black Policies Globally is truly not based on Black Culture, or the truth of Blacks. They are based off and on, White Culture, White Lies and Deceit, White Enterprise, White Economy, and more.</u>

Black People were the brainchild of civilization, now look at us. Poor and destitute because we gave up truth for lies.
We no longer own Earth thus, our lack of unity, our crab in a barrel mentality and living globally.

We say God, but how can God prepare a true home for us if we know not God?

How can God prepare a true home for is if; we do nothing to help God prepare?

It's time for us; Blacks to get off our ass and do positively for self, our children, our God, our communities globally, and our future generations.

Si dung neva sey git up. So, get up and rise decent and proper come on now. Earth can change but we as humans need to take the necessary steps for Earth to be better – change.

Michelle

It's June 28, 2020 and I am truly glad June is just about over. Like I said, June has been a month of hell for me, pain wise, family wise, and more.

Family dysfunction I am hoping is no more.

Slowly getting rid of the pain in my life family wise which is great.

I am telling you. When you get rid of stress WOW.

Friday June 26th was a testament of family disunity, family fights; squabble, family hatred, and more where I had to call the police.

Right now. It's truly great not living in fear – fear of some of my children, and children's friends. So, from yesterday, June 27 – 28 I've been cleaning. I have this renewed energy, and I am living. I feel truly young again – not limited.

Yes, it's hard to explain for me but; this change I truly needed hence, the new me. I am getting my true self back. Man do I truly love Lovey; God because, I have purpose in life again.

Trust me, when you get rid of your negatives, a whole new life open up for you in a positive way.

Listen, I have grown ass children. Some refuse good counsel, and they make your life hell literally. I've given my children the easy way in life because I know what's ahead of them future wise. Some listen, some refuse to listen. But as my last child, and first child said; *"mom you are a good mother. You did your best for all of us. The decisions of their brother is all on him. He's grown. Do not blame yourself for the decisions – poor decisions my second child has made in life,"* and they are correct, but it's a bit hard for me to accept. The words have not sunk in yet.

As a mother you can do all for your children, and some truly do not appreciate it.

They refuse to let go of the negatives in their life.
They hang on to all the negatives that hinder their true progress.

They follow bad company, and listen to people who have absolutely no where to go in life take them from truth. Those who are truly trying to secure their life, and a good future for them.

It's hard for me because my mother did try to teach me. I was stubborn, and now I see, and know the life lessons – valuable life lessons my mother was trying to teach me at a young age. Thus, my mother, and Lovey are my true stars in life all around. Both are securing me – my life all around.

Life is truly a learning process, and those who God truly love, God truly protect – save. So yes, it's hard on God when it comes to us as Black People because, some of us truly do not take telling – the teachings of Good and True Counsel.

Right now, my apartment is peaceful for the most part, and as I move forward, I have to see where life takes me financially, health wise, family wise, and more.

As for my dream world. Dreaming about fighting in the WWE. I will not get into this dream because I know when I see fighting someone is going to be sacrificed – die literally. So, I worry not about the WWE.

This morning June 28th, I dreamt I was in this land. I cannot tell you if the region was the South Pacific.

All I remember is, being around people; mainly men. The water; sea began to rise. As the sea rose, we began to run because the sea was consuming the land. We could not go high because there was no Mountain to run to. The land was flat. We kept running for safety, but the water kept coming after us. Some found not an arch but; bridge; no not bridge, but something they could stand on for the water on the ground not to consume; kill them. I truly cannot analyze this dream.

All I know is, Death is going to be by water more and more it seems. I just have to watch and see which land is ravaged by either a tsunami, earthquake and or, storms; a hurricane.

Right now, DEATH HAS COMMAND OF EARTH, AND DEATH IS GOING TO USE THEIR AUTHORITY AT WILL; KILL. We as humans made it so therefore, humans know not the TRUTH OF LIFE.

Humans truly do not think of the penalty associated with one sin; their sin, and sins.

As for us in the Black Race, we do not realize that when we go to the different churches and bow down on our knees to pray, we are not praying to God but praying to, and giving homage to Death. Therefore, God truly do not look at any church goer.

<u>*Religion is a curse thus, religion is of Death. Truly forbidden for the Children of Life to get involved with, and in.*</u>

Michelle

Thank you Lovey, it's the last day of June 2020. June be gone. Hello positivity, positive living, positive thoughts, positive buying, positive growth health wise, positive growth financially, positive eating, positive walking, positive strength, positive travels, positive everything. Absolutely nothing negative, or evil in my life Lovey. Let's truly grow together where we are not limited in anyway.

True change. No negativity ever anymore.

Lovey, tell me; what's it with Black People not wanting to know the truth?

What is so wrong with the truth?
What is so wrong with you Lovey?

What is wrong about letting go of the White Man's ways of lies, and deceit including, the lies and deceit of other nations?

I was at my dad's house yesterday until today. I am home now, and this morning I dreamt Terry Crews. **He was against me speaking the truth,** so he came after me with this long saw without (the) handle trying to kill me. At one point in the dream, I got the saw and I bent the saw to break it in half. After getting the saw and bending it to break it. Terry got another long saw to kill me. I can't remember if the saw Terry had touched the ground. _But wow Lovey to Black Americans, and what I am seeing dream wise with them._

Lovey if you want change would you not change you first?

If you need positive change for Black People, _would you not do all that is positive for yourself and Black People?_

Fighting a losing battle cannot promote change, it can only promote violence, hate; create warped people in the end.

I truly do not want to analyze this dream Lovey because I see the nature, and know the nature of Black Americans. **I cannot fight with them, nor can I fight for them.** All I can do is come to you Lovey, to let these Black People go. _It's time to truly let go of the North American and or, American Israelites._ They have no place with you so, it's time to truly let Israel go. You cannot hang on to people who truly do not know what true change is.

You deemed Judah - Jamaica unclean. So, what about Israel; the true Israelites that do all to aid evil against their Black Own?

Without true change for the better good Lovey, we will never have peace, or true peace here on Earth. We will forever be the battered and bruised; used and abused.

You have to walk away from Israel as you've walked away from Judah. Both lands have to be no more. Death must consume their true own now come on now. *Israel and Judah did turn their back on you. So, truly let these lands go. The people of these lands were fooled, now they've literally lost you.*

Further, it's time for us Lovey to undo the damage of the White Race; all the races that have and has impacted Life, and the Life of Earth, the Spiritual Realm, the Universe, and Beyond negatively.

Yes, the damage has been done here on Earth by negative; wicked and evil people; humans, but we need true change for our good and true people only Lovey. Earth cannot continue on her destructive path due to humans.

Humans are wicked to humans thus, Science; Scientist are truly the Devil's Own literally.

How can you design to kill?

How can you design, and manufacture chemicals, viruses, diseases, and more to kill?

What type of monster are you (scientists) to take life from life?

Lovey, in all you did, was this what you wanted for humans?

How did humans get so vile that they have to live to kill?

Now with this pandemic, I was thinking about the Waterways of Life. Lovey, I see the way humans discard their gloves, and face mask anywhere. Now tell me Lovey, *how many of these masks, gloves, and face coverings will find their way in the Waterways of Life due to human neglect; nastiness; uncaring ways for the environment?*

Lovey, nothing is protected in life when it comes to humans and this is truly sad.

As for my dream with Terry Crews, *what is going to happen in the United States?*

Will something split the country apart?

You know what, let me let things be because, at the end of the dream; Terry Crews dream; when I woke up out of my sleep, I did not know where I was then I realized I was at my father's home; apartment.

So yes Lovey, humans will forever continue on a destructive path because we are being controlled literally.

Yes, I was thinking about how we are controlled as well. Nothing we do is private hence the different platforms of intrusion that literally spy on us daily.

So yes, I can see a world where humans have absolutely no say because, humans matter not to those who live to control; conquer on a different level.

Humans are slaves to the different systems of men yet, none can see this because all think the bullshit the White Race is doing is good. Therefore, billions are colonized in a different way, and they truly do not know it.

It is only when we turn off the internet literally, the different television outlets, radio outlets, the different ATMs then maybe humans will see what is happening; going on in their life.

Michelle

POETRY

FREE SPIRIT

I am without a care in the world
Free from negative thoughts
Actions
You

I am me
Free to be me
Cannot be confined
Chained to society

I am a bird
Flight – fly – take flight
Free spirited
Massive

I am jovial
Not your joke
Shame
Deadly device

I am human
Organic
Will never be plastic

I am earthly
Spiritual
Universal
Heavenly

I am all I need to be for me
Not you

I have to be me
You have to be you

You cannot be me

I am me
Individual
Woman
Precise
Free

Now I ask you

What are you

Michelle Jean, May 23, and May 26, 2020

Covid-19
2020 SO FAR by Michelle Jean

Oh man this is 2020
A year for confusion
Death
Chemical, and Germ Warfare
Scare tactics
Line ups
Blame
Death

No one talking
Jobs fading
Corporations gaining
The average citizen losing

Whose to say
No one really knows
Conspiracy theories flying
People buying
Truly not thinking
Dying

Contagion
Contagion
Yes, the movie
Hence, we are being played like monopoly

Humans are the cause
Because
We are corporate and government guinea pigs

Lack of thought
Someone else doing the thinking
Choosing
Who lives
Who dies

What do you say?

Do you even care?

A jus reality

JUST REALITY – Shabba Ranks

People are not thinking
Truly living
Seeing
Listening

Thus, the reality of man is doom

The death of the races especially those in the Black Community.
We are their target
Test subject
Many not seeing
Too ignorant to see what's going on around them

Ghetto life
Ghetto lifestyle
Ghetto thought
The God spell

Nothings real anymore
Not even our Black Skin
Thus, the game
Blame game
White collar criminals that have all the say

Therefore, keep real
Truly real

Aye yes
Food shortage
Death toll rising

Many will be chipped
Their new vaccine
Well chip-cine – chip embedded in their new vaccines

No one sees
Know

Thus, many will be extinguished

It's the way
Their way
New World Order

Now you know
Stay safe

Therefore, be real
Be the good and true you you need to be for you
Your family
Friends
Beloved

Positive love of truth, and true vibration
True love always

Michelle Jean
May 23, and May 26, 2020

BLACK LIVES MATTER

Wow what a joke!
When has "Black Lives" matter?
Are we not the enemy of the state?
The guinea pigs for the different races

The used
Abused
The lynched
The one everyone kills
Hate

From Africa to North America to the Caribbean
Black Lives matter not; not even to our own.
We are just pawns
The refused
Looked down upon
Sold

We own nothing
Are treated as nothing

So, we March
Protest
Become Violent
Think all we do will make a change

But, after the Protests
Marches
The Speeches
We go right back to the same old same old.
Playing their dirty little games
Become recycled
Used
The killed again

Therefore, true change come from within

So, we wait until something else happen again
We March Again
Protest
Become violent again
Talk
Become their gimmick in systems designed to eradicate all Black Life.

Seek acceptance from those who truly hate us
Continue to want people to like us
Be fair to us

Yes, we seek change, but; no one can change the corrupt few that own the systems of White Injustice.

White Supremacy
White Lies
Fake World

CHANGES - Tupac
CHANGE YOUR LIFE - by the reggae artist Bushman

Until we as Blacks truly identify as Black, and gain some self worth, we will forever be valueless in the different systems of man.

We will forever destroy each other
Forever be our own worst enemy

We have no Black Gold
No Black Pride
No Black Identity
Black Economy
Black Industry
Black Class

Everything is Race
So, we bypass
Claim to be but aren't because, we truly do not know the truth of our past
Our Roots
Black Civilizations
Yes, our true Black Life

So, we seek to find
Yet cannot find

We become brainwashed
Play their dirty games
Become blind, and ignorant to the truth around
Truly think people care; give a damn

So, we change
Seek to belong in their corrupt systems of lies, and deceit
Live in the dark

Still do not truly know that we do not belong in the different Systems of Man – the White Man.

Racism
Bah
It's my right not to like you.

It's my God given right not to like you either as long as I do not hurt you, do things to harm, and kill you.

So, truly do not force me to like you, or accept you

Thus, no one can seek truth; fairness in unjust societies that has and have left them in the dark literally.

Societies that defame us
Take our truth from us
Cast Blacks as uneducated
Rob us of our true roots
Heritage
History

So why should Black Life Matter when we take life from self, take our Blackness for granted, have absolutely no respect for self, and each other.

So, we sit
We talk
Become fools for those who truly hate us

We even think our Marches, violent protests matters

Where is our true Black Economy?
Hospitals
Banks
Auto Industry

True Black Leaders who have not sold out to the highest bidder; are not corporate, and government owned.

Black devils who are pitted against their own people
Are used to blindside, and rape their own Black People

When we have a true Black Wall Street then we can talk. So truly don't talk to me about Black Lives because, all I have to do is look at the state of every Black Community Globally, and show you that Black Lives truly do not matter.

But for those who hate and kill us; use us as pawns, Black Lives Matter. But to us, Black Lives will never matter to us as a people and true society because, we continually fall for their games; traps.

Black on Black Crime
Black infection rate – diseases – death
Lack of Black Unity
Lack of Blacks truly supporting our own

White Psychology that has pit Blacks against Blacks to the point where some beach their skin to look white – dead.

Black ghettos
Black poverty
Lack of civility
Our hidden agenda of self destruction
Self Hate
The Slave Game

So, with all this said, how can Black Lives Matter when you have no hope?
Growth for the future
Good assets to leave behind for our future generations
Children
Community
You

Have we not defamed those before us who have died for Black Rights? Civil Rights

So, tell me, HOW WE LIVING WHEN WE'VE SHAMED THOSE BEFORE US THAT HAS AND HAVE FOUGHT FOR BLACK RIGHTS.

None know that; violence begets violence.
Looked down upon

And, the only way to hurt our enemies is to hurt them in their pocket book.
Truly buy Black.

Michelle Jean
June 8, 2020
Edited June 16, 2020

BOOKS WRITTEN BY MICHELLE JEAN – 2020

FIRST BOOK OF 2020

BOOK TWO 2020

JUST ONE OF THOSE DAYS 2020

TRUTH – THE MONTH OF TRUTH – FEBRUARY 2020 AND BEYOND

ENGLAND – MANKIND

I DON'T KNOW BUT I DO

CANDIDLY SPEAKING LOVEY

THE COMPLEXITY OF LIFE – CONFUSION

2020 SO FAR